Beth and Trish like the beach.
Many things wash up there.
They see shells, rocks, and fish.

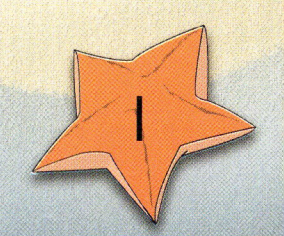

1

One day, Beth and Trish saw a trunk.
It was black.
It had sunk down in the sand.

"How will we get it out?" asked Trish.
Beth tried to pick it up.
The trunk was too slick.

The trunk was stuck.
"I wish it would move," said Beth.
Then the trunk moved!

4

"Did you see that?" asked Trish.
The trunk had moved.
It was not stuck.

The trunk was locked.
"I wish it would open," said Beth.
Then the lock fell on the sand!

SCREECH!

The trunk lid fell back.

"Quick! Reach inside," said Trish.

The trunk was full of rings and things.
Trish yelled, "What great luck!"
They had found a treasure trunk.